Original title:
Berry Good Times

Copyright © 2025 Creative Arts Management OÜ
All rights reserved.

Author: Miriam Kensington
ISBN HARDBACK: 978-1-80586-271-0
ISBN PAPERBACK: 978-1-80586-743-2

Seasons of Sweetness

Winter's chill, a frosty bite,
Dreams of fruit take wing in flight.
Springtime blooms, a burst of cheer,
Juicy surprises linger near.

Summer sun, oh what a treat,
Splashing juice on hungry feet.
Autumn's harvest, colors bright,
Time for pie and pure delight.

Palette of Pinks and Purples

Pinks and purples, hues so bold,
Every fruit, a tale retold.
Blushing cheeks of ripe delight,
Giggles shared, oh what a sight!

In a patch, the laughter flows,
Plucking snacks as friendship grows.
Nature's canvas, sweet and ripe,
Painting moments, pure of type.

Luminescent Fruits

Shiny globes of pure delight,
Glowing under moon's soft light.
Slippery hands, we all will slip,
Juicy bites make laughter drip.

Peeking out from leafy greens,
A jester's prank, or so it seems.
Every bite, a burst of fun,
A fruity party, never done!

Enchanted Harvest

In a field where giggles grow,
Wobbling fruits put on a show.
Chasing shadows, race we will,
With laughter high, my heart to fill.

Magic moments, hand in hand,
Fruity wonders, oh so grand.
Every scoop and chaos reigns,
In this harvest, joy remains.

Whispers of the Orchard

In a grove where laughter grows,
Fruits wear hats, in fancy shows.
Cherries jiggle on sweet breeze,
Peaches giggle as they tease.

Lemons scheme with playful zest,
Raspberry rhymes, the very best.
Orchard whispers tales of cheer,
Where every tree shakes off the fear.

Fields of Flavor

Fields alive with sleepy dreams,
Strawberry hats, and juice that streams.
Pickles dance with smirking glee,
Winking cucumbers, wild and free.

Lemonade lakes are quite the sight,
Berries soaring like kites in flight.
Nature giggles, oh so sly,
As pickled pumpkins wave goodbye.

The Dance of Juicy Joy

Fruits are twirling, all around,
In a circus where laughs abound.
Bananas peel with daring flair,
While grapes are giggling in the air.

Melons roll like clowns at play,
Juicy joy is here to stay.
With every bounce, more smiles soar,
In a carnival of taste galore.

Nature's Candy

Sugar dreams on every vine,
Nature's sweets are quite divine.
Funky flavors, bold and bright,
Tickle tongues and hearts ignite.

Frolic through the candy patch,
Where flavors laugh, and fruits all match.
Jellybeans in joyful bloom,
A sweet parade that lifts the gloom.

Taste of Nature's Blessing

In a patch where giggles grow,
Red and round, they steal the show.
Juicy laughter fills the air,
Nature's candy, beyond compare.

With a splash of cream so bright,
Splat! The kids are in delight.
Sticky fingers, joyful screams,
Every bite, a tasty dream.

Racing to see who'll get the most,
Sticky smiles, we laugh and boast.
In the sun, we dance and play,
Fruit-filled joys make our day.

When the sun begins to dip,
We'll gather all, then take a sip.
Nature's feast, a funny sight,
Turning twilight into night.

Cherished Harvests

In fields where mischief grows,
A fruity fight, as everyone knows.
Splat! A splash of fruity goo,
Watch your step or you'll slip too!

Tiny hands dive and dive,
Searching for the treat to thrive.
With every giggle, fruits collide,
A berry bonanza, oh what a ride!

Tickle fights with every pick,
Jelly stains, we go for quick.
Running wild, hearts in sync,
Nature's joy makes us all wink.

As night falls with stars so bright,
We'll share our treasures, what a sight!
Each little laugh, a cherished prize,
Harvests of fun before our eyes.

Juice of Laughter

In the kitchen, chaos reigns,
Fruit flies dance, here come the gains.
Blender roars, a wild refrain,
Splashing juice, oh what a stain!

Friends gather round, laughter flows,
Sticky fingers, everybody knows.
Tasting mishaps, oh what a show,
We can't help but laugh and glow.

Sweet Summer's Embrace

Picnic blankets scattered wide,
Silly hats, we wear with pride.
Juicy slices on the side,
Melon mayhem, our goofy ride!

Sunshine rays, they tickle our skin,
In this food fight, who will win?
Splattered laughter, cheeky grins,
Squeals of joy as the fun begins!

Ripe Moments Unfolding

Under trees with shady arms,
We pick the fruit, it works like charms.
Ripe and squishy, they cause alarms,
Juice drips down, with all its harms!

A plop, a drop, we can't refrain,
Nature's mess, oh what a gain!
We giggle loud, despite the pain,
Sticky shoes, our playful bane.

Nature's Juicy Whispers

In the garden, giggles grow,
Nature whispers secrets low.
Each cherry picked puts on a show,
With every bite, our faces glow!

Worms and ants join in the fun,
Underneath the blazing sun.
Sharing tales till day is done,
Who knew picking could outrun?

Vibrance in the Meadow

In the field, laughter sways,
Sunshine dances, bright displays.
Bouncing blooms, a colors' race,
Nature's joy, a happy place.

Bees in suits, they do a jig,
Chasing dreams, they're feeling big.
With petals soft, they play and roam,
In this meadow, call it home.

A Bounty to Remember

Plums and peaches share a grin,
Giggling fruits, a joyful spin.
Pie in hand, we take a seat,
With that slice, who can be beat?

Sticky hands from all the sweets,
Run through fields on happy feet.
Laughing loud, we share our finds,
Creating laughs of all kinds.

Whispers of Wild Harvest

Under trees where secrets sleep,
Wild delights that make us leap.
Ticklish leaves, a teasing breeze,
Nature's joke, oh what a tease!

Squirrels giggle, stealing bites,
Stashing snacks from morning flights.
As crowns of thorns adorn our heads,
Running wild on nature's beds.

Radiant Rubies in the Sun

Glistening gems, we find our way,
Sipping sun on a hot day.
Juicy laughter bursts and flows,
Berry treasures, nature shows.

Fruits parade with wobbly glee,
Cooling off under the tree.
Sipping juice, we make a toast,
To these moments we love most.

Sweetness on the Wind

Fragrant whispers dance and sway,
Tickling noses on a sunny day.
Giggles float on a breeze so light,
Chasing shadows, what a delight!

Laughter bubbles, bright and loud,
Underneath the cotton-cloud.
Silly hats and running shoes,
Swapping tales of sweetly hues.

Fields of Laughter

In a meadow where the fun does bloom,
Cuckoo calls in the afternoon.
Dance with daisies, turn around,
Tickle your toes on the grassy ground.

In the distance, a kite does glide,
While giggling friends come side by side.
Caught in a web of playful cheer,
Chasing each other, never fear!

Plucking Dreams from the Bush

In the thicket, a treasure hides,
With winks and nudges, excitement rides.
Handfuls of joy plucked with glee,
Squirrels giggle as they scurry free.

Sticky fingers, laughter shared,
Smiles exchanged, nobody cared.
The bushes sing with a playful jive,
In this wild patch, we come alive!

Juiced Joy

Squeeze the fun from every drop,
Laughter bubbles, never stop.
Fruity flavors swirl and mix,
Sips of joy, a tasty fix!

Lemonade laughter, sweetness bright,
Giddy moments, pure delight.
Friends all gather in a row,
Pouring memories, watch them flow!

Golden Days

Sunshine glistens on the cheek,
Every moment feels unique.
Chasing twilight, dancing spry,
Underneath the painted sky.

Moments linger in the air,
With each chuckle, show you care.
Golden hours drift and sway,
Here's to laughter—hip hooray!

Savoring the Sweetness

In the garden of juicy dreams,
A chubby squirrel plots his schemes.
With ripe delights falling down,
He wears a berry crown, a feathery gown.

Giggling buds dance in the breeze,
Tickling imagination with ease.
Each flavor is a little prank,
Even the bees can't help but prank!

So come and taste the rich collide,
With comrades on this fruity ride.
A splash of laughter drips like jam,
Life's a jolly, blooming slam!

In every bite, a joke resides,
Each sour face brings chuckles wide.
With goofy twists and silly quirks,
We savor life in these little perks.

Fruitful Adventures

Jumping into the vibrant fields,
Where laughter's harvest never yields.
Swinging from a tangy vine,
Adventurous taste is truly divine!

Splat! A plum just whizzed on by,
Oh no, it's flying high in the sky!
Chasing fruits with silly glee,
What a silly sight to see!

With every zip, a fruity fling,
Full of giggles, oh what a swing!
The squirrels chime in with a cheer,
While wearin' hats made of...pear?

So grab a buddy, don't be shy,
In juicy realms, let's laugh and fly.
Together we'll make the harvest swell,
With fruity tales, we'll weave our spell!

Lush Laughter

In a world of color, bright and bold,
Giggles pop like fruit on hold.
Juicy jokes hang from each limb,
A fruity pun that's sure to swim!

Cherries blush as they hear the jest,
While watermelon plays host to the fest.
Don't forget the zesty lime,
Making sour faces quite sublime!

Gather 'round the citrus swell,
Where laughter's juice begins to yell.
Banana peels play the fool,
In this fruity kingdom, life's the rule!

So toast your cups with sprightly cheer,
To laughter flowing, oh so near.
With every sip, joy rain cascades,
In fruity realms, we're never fades!

Bounty of Bliss

In a luscious land of sunshine smiles,
Each fruit brings giggles for miles.
Jelly beans dance in a line,
While maraschino dreams shine so fine!

Chomp down on a chuckleberry crunch,
As silliness unfolds in every munch.
Grapes in a cluster, tease so loud,
Making merry with the giggling crowd!

With every pluck, there's laughter shared,
In this orchard, we all dared.
Spinach in a berry disguise,
Whispers secrets with silly eyes!

So join this fruity, zany ball,
With each delight, we'll have a ball.
Bouncing joy in every bite,
This harvest is pure delight!

Tart Surprises in the Shade

In the canopy where shadows play,
A fruit fell down without delay.
I squealed with laughter, that little gnome,
Turns out he was just looking for home.

Wobbly knee, I tried to bend,
Lured by pie, my best of friends.
But tripped on roots and made a scene,
Now I'm the jester, a fool routine.

Dancing ants and flies so bold,
Tasting sweet, but it turned moldy gold.
Who knew a picnic could end so wild?
With squishy fruit, I squeaked and smiled.

Squeezed juices dripped on my shirt,
Oh, the sticky mess, it didn't hurt.
We laughed till we cried, what a fabulous ruckus,
Nature's jest, in the shade, a circus!

Handpicked Happiness

With baskets swinging, we set the pace,
Counting laughing fits in a berry-laden race.
Plucking joy from thorny vines,
Each bite a giggle, oh how it shines!

A sly raccoon peeked from behind a branch,
Took a berry, gave us quite the chance!
Chasing it down, we lost our hats,
Stumbling over bushes, oh look at that!

Splattered faces, with juice we're dressed,
"Who wore it better?" was the funny quest.
Nature's confetti, all over the ground,
Our laughter echoed, delight profound!

In the end, all we gathered was cheer,
With sticky fingers and hearts sincere.
Handpicked happiness, each one's a must,
Forever binding, in fruit we trust!

Petals and Plums

In gardens where petal rain does fall,
We danced under trees, feeling quite small.
A whiff of plums got tangled in air,
And suddenly, we were without a care!

Fluffy clouds of laughter swirl,
As friends in pigtails begin to twirl.
Diving for fruit, we feast on delight,
A funny sweet frenzy, a comical sight!

Tiny critters joined in our bliss,
With buzzing wings, they wouldn't miss.
We shared our plunder; oh what a thrill,
Together in joy, our hearts to fill!

But nature played a cheeky prank,
With juicy splats, we fell in rank.
Covered in bits, we roared with glee,
Petals and plums, life's party spree!

Sunkissed Joys

Under the sun, warm and bright,
Banana peels made for quite the sight!
We slipped and slid, a comical crew,
With laughter erupting, we all knew!

On a treasure hunt for goodies galore,
Who knew squash could be such a chore?
We shouted and rolled, our spirits so high,
Amidst funny mishaps, we learned to fly!

Sunkissed joys on this wobbly spree,
Each fallen fruit a sweet jubilee.
Giggles bubbled up, we danced on the green,
Brightly alive, our souls a sheen!

As daylight faded, we claimed the stage,
In sticky glory, we had our wage.
With our silly tales, we'll laugh till we're blue,
Sunkissed moments, forever true!

Sweet Symphony of the Seasons

In June we danced with cherries bright,
Their sweetness matched our sheer delight.
With every bite, a giggle grew,
Each fruit a note, our joy the cue.

But in July, oh how they fell,
Strawberries bursting, a juicy spell.
We slipped and slid on the berry goo,
Laughter echoed, like summer's hue.

August brought the plums so bold,
We juggled them, so brave and bold.
They squished and splashed, what a sight,
We laughed till dark, then danced 'til night.

As autumn waves its golden hand,
We toast with apples, ripe and grand.
With cider sips and silly pranks,
Our hearts so light, our laughter ranks.

Portraits of Pleasures

A canvas bright with fruits so rare,
Mango smiles in tropical air.
With peaches' charm and humor's tease,
We painted joy with every breeze.

Next on the palette, grapes entwined,
We fumbled and tumbled, laughter aligned.
Hilarity bloomed while we had fun,
Our giggles echoed, like rays of sun.

Bananas split, a slapstick cheer,
As slip and slide drew all near.
We took our poses, silly and bright,
Creating memories, pure delight.

With every fruit a tale untold,
We shared our joy, both young and old.
In this art of laughter, we remain,
Forever painted in the joy of gain.

Nectarous Narratives

Once upon a time, in a berry patch,
A squirrel appeared, a comical catch.
He wriggled and jiggled, all in delight,
As blueberries flew, what a silly sight!

Then came the bear, looking for lunch,
He sniffed and grunted, a funny hunch.
With honey drips, he danced around,
While visions of fruit filled his mind with sound.

Raspberries giggled as they rolled away,
While strawberries chuckled, refusing to stay.
Each flaunted their colors, oh what a game!
In this tale of fruit, none were the same.

As twilight fell, the critters sang,
In harmony, sweet fruit-flavored clang.
And in that patch, where laughter soared,
They lived out their tales, forever adored.

Fruitful Gatherings

Gather round, it's time to feast,
With every fruit, we claim the least.
Peaches plump and donuts bright,
Rolling on dough, what a delight!

Next came lemons, mischief's muse,
We slipped on zest, in playful snooze.
With lemonade showers, sweet and sour,
We danced in joy, hour by hour.

Then cherries dropped from trees so tall,
We dodged and laughed, no fear of a fall.
With faces smeared in sticky bliss,
Each bite a secret, a fruity kiss.

At sun's end, with fruit-stained hands,
We shared our tales, in merry bands.
A party of laughter, nonsense and cheer,
In every fruit, we found our dear.

Fields of Exuberance

In a patch of laughter, berries grow,
Outrageous colors, putting on a show.
They giggle and dance, as children shout,
With every bite, there's a joyous rout.

Sunshine bursts on every cheek,
Sticky fingers, fruit's mystique.
A raspberry jumps, the others cheer,
Rolling off the table like they have no fear.

Grinning faces, dripping juice,
Never mind the funny excuse.
A fruit fight breaks, chaos in flight,
Squeezed giggles under sunlight bright.

The harvest ends with smiles galore,
Pies and jellies, and oh, so much more.
In this field of fun, we claim our prize,
With berry-splattered clothes, we laugh and rise.

Juicy Juxtaposition

A cherry whispers to a cantaloupe,
"Together we're quite the fragrant hope."
Lemons crack jokes with a creamy scoop,
While raspberries giggle, joining the troupe.

Some pick a fight, a juicy brawl,
Watermelons wobble, making folks fall.
Strawberries blush, embarrassed in shade,
As blueberries watch from the cool cascade.

Fruits wear hats, so quirky and bright,
A pineapple swaggers, full of delight.
Old fruits chat about past sweet days,
Tarot grapefruit reads through breakfast phase.

But who knows, with zest we might find,
A twist of flavor, one of a kind.
A party of fruits, all wild and free,
In this juicy mix, come dance with me!

Colorful Constellations

Under the stars, fruits start to plot,
A citrus comet, they twist in a lot.
Blackberries rumble, their laughter loud,
While starfruit winks from a fluffy cloud.

A blueberry moon lights up the night,
Kiwis and oranges, poised for flight.
They swirl in tango, laughter in space,
Creating a galaxy of fruity grace.

Tartness and sweetness dance on the tongue,
Old mango tales, forever sung.
Pineapples gossip, so juicy and round,
As cherry confetti rains on the ground.

In the sky, they twinkle, pure allure,
A cosmic blend, a taste so sure.
For in this universe, so bright and vast,
Every fruit's friendship holds a memory cast.

Whirling Whispers of Fruit

In the orchard's heart, secrets unfold,
With whispers of sweetness, both brave and bold.
Grapes giggle as they tumble down,
Joining the fun in a wild fruit town.

Here comes a peach with a twinkle in eye,
"Let's roll down the hill, oh my, oh my!"
Lemons and limes, they trip and fall,
Creating a ruckus, balancing all.

Plum jokes around, a flexible chap,
While apricots tease from a fuzzy gap.
Bananas slip-slide in a playful doodle,
Making a ruckus, oh what a noodle!

The fruit brigade is an uproarious blur,
With laughter and juices, they stutter and stir.
In this whirling world of fruity delight,
Come join their capers, under moonlight!

Picnics in Paradise

We spread our blanket wide and free,
While ants march forth as if to see.
The sandwiches hide from our wild glee,
And juice boxes squirt with wild esprit.

Checkered cloth and laughter blend,
As laughter's echo will not end.
A squirrel sneaks up but won't pretend,
He's sharing food like a good friend.

The lemonade spills, oh what a scene!
We yell at the bugs, so mean yet keen.
With every mishap, we laugh and gleen,
Picnic chaos, the best cuisine!

As the sun dips low, we gather cheer,
With giggles and slices of pie on sphere.
In this wild feast, we raise a beer,
And toast to joy, with friends so dear.

Sweet Smiles and Sunshine

Under the rays, we grin so wide,
With fruit in hand, we cannot hide.
A watermelon slice, a juicy ride,
Laughter swirls like a playful tide.

Sun-kissed cheeks and a cherry pit,
We toss it far, oh what a hit!
Sticky fingers from each tasty bit,
In this sweet moment, we all fit.

The sun dances on our silly hats,
As we chase after playful cats.
Tickled by rays, there's no time for spats,
Just giggles and snacks, oh where are the mats?

With bubbles floating in the breeze,
We squeal as we feel the summer tease.
Our hearts are light, our spirits seize,
In this sweet sun, we're just a tease.

Juicy Tales of the Field

Gather round for tales so sweet,
Of plump fruit we cannot beat.
In fields where laughter and mischief meet,
We tripped on vines, oh what a feat!

Once there was a berry that was shy,
It hid from us up in the sky.
But with a little coaxing made it fly,
Now it sings songs, oh my oh my!

We plucked a peach, it took a dive,
And bounced right back as we all jive.
With every bite, we felt alive,
This juicy chaos, oh what a strive!

So grab your friends, let's make some noise,
With fruit galore, we'll feast in joys.
In every bop and every poise,
These tales of juice bring heart to poise.

Flavorful Freedoms

In the garden where flavors bloom,
We pick and munch, there's no room for gloom.
Tasting sweetness, a joyful boom,
As nature's bounty fills our room.

With every sip of tangy zest,
We dance around, feeling the best.
Cracking jokes, we're truly blessed,
In fruity chaos, we never rest.

Swirls of cream and dashes bright,
We craft a feast, a pure delight.
With every laugh, we take a bite,
Flavorful freedom, our hearts ignite.

As night descends with stars so bold,
We share our stories, laughter untold.
In this flavorful dance, we feel gold,
United by fun, forever sold.

Nature's Symphony

In the garden where colors gleam,
Fruits dance like they're in a dream.
The sun shines bright, what a sight,
Chasing shadows with pure delight.

Bees buzzing like a joyful tune,
Tickling petals, they hum and swoon.
Laughter echoes through the trees,
As they flirt with the playful breeze.

Each drop of dew a gem so rare,
Nature's treasure, all laid bare.
Unruly vines in joyful plight,
Make mischief from morning till night.

Underneath the apple's shade,
Silly moments are paraded.
With plump pink cheeks, we take a bite,
Oh, the sweetness — what pure delight!

Sweet Nectar of Life

A potluck feast on a sunny hill,
Juicy jewels, oh what a thrill!
From raspberry reds to blueberry blues,
Each flavor a laugh, we can't refuse.

Sticky fingers, playful glee,
Fruit splatters, wild and free.
Munching snacks, trying not to choke,
As the wind plays trickster, what a joke!

With every bite, giggles arise,
Silly faces, to our surprise.
A playful toss, a fruit-filled flight,
This is the joy we crave each night.

Wrapped in sweetness, we sway and spin,
Cherishing every messy grin.
In this banquet of mirth so rife,
Who knew laughter would be our life?

Aromas of Abundance

In fields alive with scents so sweet,
Nature's perfume leads us to greet.
The warming sun, a wink of fun,
As we giggle in this endless run.

With every whiff, a chuckle bursts,
Those fruity aromas, we crave first.
Sun-kissed delights in every nook,
A fruity surprise comes from every crook.

Colors splash like paint on a page,
Each taste we take, ignites a stage.
With friends beside, we leap and roll,
Every mouthful fills our soul.

Underneath the umbrella shade,
Silly dances in the charade.
As flavor hits, our giggles rise,
Savoring joy in sweet surprise!

Whims of the Wild

The wild whispers tall tales and lies,
Fruitful adventures under bright skies.
Dancing squirrels, a sight to see,
Join us in this revelry!

With every toss, shadows dance too,
Laughter twirls in zesty view.
Wildflower crowns with stems entwined,
A goofy bunch, so well-defined.

Underneath the leafy crown,
Silly antics never drown.
In playful skips and hasty dashes,
We gather dreams amid the clashes.

So let's convene where bright fruits glow,
And let our giggles steal the show.
In this enchanted, playful land,
Life's hilarious tales, hand in hand!

Tart and Tantalizing

In a patch of sun, they gleam,
Sour faces, sweetened dream.
Chasing flavors with a grin,
Sour vs. sweet, let the games begin!

Taste buds dance, a wild flight,
Lemon drop, or cherry bite?
Laughs erupt with each surprise,
Pucker up, oh what a prize!

Sticky fingers, juice in streams,
Sipping sunshine, bursting beams.
Who knew that tart could be so fun,
Sun-drenched pickin', everyone!

Giggling kids in a berry maze,
Making memories in a daze.
With every scoop, joy unfolds,
Tart adventures in vivid folds!

Dewdrop Dreams

Morning light, a sparkling haze,
Dewdrop jewels in sunlit bays.
Fruit hangs low with a cheeky grin,
Inviting all to dive right in!

Bouncing laughter, oh what a sight,
Juicy secrets, pure delight.
Nature's party in each sphere,
A taste explosion, never fear!

Sipping nectar in warm embrace,
Sticky paws, a wild chase.
Tickled toes in grass below,
A dewy dance, go with the flow!

Chasing flavors, round and round,
Flavor fireworks, joy is found.
In every drop, dreams take flight,
Nature's laughter, pure delight!

The Color of Flavor

Painted scenes of red and blue,
Tasting rainbows, how about you?
Splatters of joy in every bite,
Colors bursting, pure delight!

Pick a hue, then take a chance,
Each bite's a flavor dance!
Orange or green? Take a lick,
Tastebud magic, quick, quick, quick!

Gobbling up the jewel-toned treats,
Laughing as the sweet stuff greets.
Nature's palette in every nibble,
With every crunch, we giggle and dribble!

Who knew taste could be so bright?
A fruity frenzy, oh what a sight!
In every color, fun unfolds,
The color of flavor, stories told!

Nature's Succulent Secrets

Hidden gems in leafy palaces,
Secrets whispered through sweet chalices.
Mysterious fruits, wild and free,
Nature's candy, come see, come see!

Bouncing between branches and leaves,
Tasting treasures that nature gives.
With a giggle and playful race,
Each flavor found, a sweet embrace!

Raspberry smiles, a fruity feast,
Gather the sweetness, it never ceased.
Laughter echoes through the trees,
Nature plays, with flavors that tease!

From every cranny, juice descends,
Sipping sunshine, time transcends.
Exploring nature's juicy realms,
With every bite, joy overwhelms!

Luscious Landscapes

In fields awash with colorful hues,
The critters dance, they've paid their dues.
Red, blue, and green, oh what a sight,
Nature's laughter, pure delight.

The squirrels plan their berry heist,
While rabbits munch, oh how they feist.
A feast laid out, no need for a plate,
In these landscapes, it's all first-rate.

The wind tickles leaves, a playful tease,
Nature's buffet, as easy as you please.
Birds swoop down, on a mission so sly,
Stealing fruits as they zip by.

With every bite, a giggle is shared,
In this paradise, nobody's scared.
So join the fun, don't miss the rewards,
In these luscious lands, raise your gourds!

Harvest of Delight

When the sun shines bright and the sky's so blue,
You know it's time for the harvest crew.
With buckets in hand and smiles so wide,
We gather the fruits, joy our guide.

Oh, look at Jim, he's tripped on a vine,
Dancing in dirt, claiming it's fine.
While Mary juggles, oh what a sight,
Fruits flying high, oh what a flight!

Neighbors all laugh at the chaos below,
As berries roll out in a wild show.
Right here in the fields, we find such bliss,
Harvesting joy, we can't miss.

With baskets of laughter, we head to the stand,
Selling sweet smiles, isn't life grand?
Each customer leaves with a grin, oh so wide,
In this harvest of delight, we all take pride.

Nature's Festivity

Amidst fields wearing fruit hats so bright,
Nature throws a party, what a delight!
With leaves as confetti, they flutter and play,
As giggles echo, chasing clouds away.

The bees all buzz, a cheerful band,
While ants march in lines, oh so planned.
Berries bounce in the baskets with glee,
Join in the fun, come sing with me!

A picnic spreads on a cheeky green mound,
Humor and flavor in every bite found.
With laughter as seasoning, it's quite a treat,
Nature's festivity, can't be beat!

So twirl like a fruit, let worries float by,
Under the sun and a laughing sky.
In this carnival of color, fun reigns supreme,
Life is a dance, it's all just a dream.

Ripple Effects of Sweetness

In a pool of jam, the laughter spreads wide,
Rippling echoes of sweetness collide.
The toads start croaking a silly old tune,
As the sun grins down from a fluffy white balloon.

With splashes of juice that paint the bright air,
Each drop a giggle, without a care.
Squirrels do somersaults, showing their flair,
In this silly wonder, oh, nothing can compare.

The fruits do dance, with their juice gushing free,
Creating delight like a zesty spree.
With every chuckle, new promises bloom,
In this rippled scene, joy finds room.

So grab a spoon, come taste the cheer,
In the playground of flavors, everyone's here.
With each burst of fun, a sweet memory stays,
In these rippling moments, laughter plays.

SorrRow Sips

In the garden, a drink spills,
Giggles bounce off the nearby hills.
Strawberries dance on the rim,
While cherries blush; oh, what a whim!

Lips stained red from too much cheer,
Glasses clink, "No worry, dear!"
Sideways smiles and silly grins,
Toasts to laughter and all our sins!

Wobbly chairs in the noon heat,
Someone's hat, a fruity treat.
Lemonade fights, fruit flies sing,
Hilarity is our king!

As the sun begins to dip,
We gather round for one more sip.
For every chuckle in our hearts,
A fruity memory never departs!

The Joyful Pick

Out in fields, we toil and play,
Picking fruits throughout the day.
Ripe delights in every hand,
A berry patch, oh, so grand!

Rolling baskets, laughter loud,
Fruits piled high, we feel so proud.
Squishy toes in juicy mud,
Hope no one slips in the gooey flood.

Threading vines, we tell our tales,
Of mishaps, hiccups, snappy gales.
Each berry stuck, a story told,
With giggles that never grow old.

Underneath the sun's warm glare,
We make a mess, without a care.
With every bite, joy we find,
A delicious day, perfectly designed!

Essence of the Earth's Gifts

In gardens lush, the treasures grow,
Nature's laughter, don't you know?
Raspberry patches hide and seek,
Juicy reds make the heart speak.

Rolling in sweet leaf debris,
A hidden cherry, just for me!
Stumbling funny, no one minds,
It's the sweetness that binds.

Flavor explosions, taste buds cheer,
Sharing notes of joy, we hear.
In every risk of sticky hands,
Adventure lies in fruity lands.

Sunset glows, the harvest's done,
We're wiping faces, oh what fun!
With every giggle and taste explored,
Earth's kind gifts, forever adored!

Flavorful Fables

Once upon a time, in a jam,
Fruits conspired with a silly plan.
Blueberries wore crowns, strawberries danced,
In the kingdom of juiciness, all pranced.

Laughing fruits held a big feast,
Inviting friends, to say the least.
Plum pies on treetops, oh so sweet,
With nectar flowing in every seat.

Tall tales of soft, sugary dreams,
Marshmallow clouds and raspberry streams.
We sip from goblets, laughter so bright,
In the land of flavor, all feels right.

And as the night falls with a sigh,
Fruit tales linger under the sky.
With giggles and joy, our hearts take flight,
Forever chasing that fruity delight!

A Feast for the Heart

In a garden bright and bold,
Laughter sprinkles, stories told.
Cakes and pies with fruity flair,
Stirring joy that fills the air.

Friends all gather, snacks in hand,
Tickled toes in sun-kissed sand.
A splash of juice, a splash of fun,
Happiness shines, we race and run.

Chasing shadows, giggles soar,
Every nibble begs for more.
Oh, the antics that unfold,
As we feast on tales retold.

When bellies ache from too much cheer,
We roll like fruit down to the pier.
With crumbs that glisten on our face,
This hearty feast, a warm embrace.

Nature's Colorful Chorus

Sunlight beams on leaves of green,
A rainbow burst, such sights unseen.
Strawberries wink, they tease and shine,
Melons giggle, tasting divine.

The bees are dancing, what a show,
They buzz and hum, just like a pro.
Daisies nod, the daisies grin,
As we munch, the fun begins.

Hiccups follow every bite,
As laughter echoes, taking flight.
Fruit juice splashes on our clothes,
In the woods where mischief grows.

Nature sings, oh, what a treat,
With every flavor, life's so sweet.
In this playful, vivid dream,
We're the stars, we gleam and beam.

Stained Fingers and Smiles

Fingers sticky, faces bright,
Juicy treasures bring delight.
Raspberry stains like tiny art,
Red on cheeks, we're set apart.

Giggles echo through the grass,
Racing each other, oh, what a class!
Kites are flying, colors swirl,
Chasing after the swirl and twirl.

When the jar tips, oh dear me!
A sticky flood, oh what a spree!
Squeals of laughter fill the air,
As fruity battles turn to fare.

With each bite, a humorous tale,
A cheerful jest we can't curtail.
So let the juice run wild and free,
In this sweet and silly jubilee!

Aroma of Sun-Kissed Days

Whiffs of sugar, scents so sweet,
Dancing breezes, life's a treat.
Sunshine warms the giggles here,
Fruity fragrances, all near.

A picnic spread on the hilltop high,
Flyaway hats that kiss the sky.
Crispy chips with a splash of zest,
Filled with laughter, we feel blessed.

Cherries tumble from each hand,
Splatters brighten up the land.
As we play and tease around,
The joy of summer's laughter found.

With every sip, we swirl and sway,
Life feels perfect in this play.
Under the sun, we'll laugh and sway,
Savoring moments that brighten our day.

A Symphony of Sweets

A fruity band plays in the sun,
With giggles and jests, oh what fun!
Jams dancing happily on toast,
While sugar plums laugh, they boast.

Raspberry tart takes the lead,
Strawberry notes fulfill our need.
Lemon drops serve as the beat,
Cheery solos, oh so sweet!

All fruits unite in a joyful tune,
Banana slips with a big balloon.
The cherry choirs sing loud and clear,
In this symphony, we shed a tear.

Round and round, the flavors sway,
In this fruity party, we play!
So raise your glass of juice with glee,
For fruit-filled laughter, come join me!

Orchard of Memories

A stroll through trees, the laughter flows,
Underneath where the wild grape grows.
Tickling leaves and grassy trails,
As we share gossip and silly tales.

Plums wobble like jelly on the vine,
Chasing fireflies, we sip sweet wine.
The sun sets low, painting the sky,
As giggles echo, oh my, oh my!

Nostalgic bites of pie, we try,
With crumbly crust that makes us sigh.
Laughter explodes like the juiciest fruit,
In this orchard, we give a hoot!

Memories hang heavy like cider's smell,
As we toast to fruits, oh what a swell!
Let's pick more laughs and savor the night,
In our orchard of joy, everything's right.

Tangy Revelations

Oh, lime, so zesty with a twist,
A citrus secret we can't resist.
Grapefruits whisper behind closed doors,
While sour faces tumble on floors.

Pineapple's truth, a prickly story,
With a hearty laugh in all its glory.
Orange peels slip on the floor,
Tangy jests, who could ask for more?

Under the sun, the fruits conspire,
With every giggle, they never tire.
Lemons laugh in a tart surprise,
As we savor truth between the lies.

So when life gives you a funny taste,
Embrace the tang, don't let it waste!
In a world so juicy and absurd,
We find joy in every word!

Luscious Moments

In a patch of laughter, we toss and spin,
Drifting through fields, let the fun begin!
Peaches drop with a squishy sound,
As joyous giggles bounce all around.

Juicy bites of mischief we savor,
Cherries on top of our whimsical flavor.
Mangoes wiggle in their bright gowns,
While we dance about without any frowns.

Whipped cream clouds float high above,
With chocolate syrup, we spread the love.
Banana splits cause a silly fight,
In this luscious dream, everything's right!

So take a slice of silly delight,
Bite into life, make it bright!
With every scoop, let laughter bloom,
In these luscious moments, there's always room.

Feast of the Wild Harvest

In the garden where the laughter grows,
Strawberries peek where the wild winds blow.
Raspberries dance with a cheeky grin,
As rabbits hop in with a playful spin.

Jam jars ready for a messy affair,
Splatters and giggles fill the sweet air.
Blueberries tumble in a squishy race,
Pies are flipped with a floury face.

Lemonade spills in a sugary stream,
The sun overhead shines like a dream.
Everyone's munching with jam on their chin,
In this feast, let the fun begin!

Pickles and cherries in a jingle bell jar,
We twirl and we whirl like a wild candy star.
So grab a spoon, let's dig down deep,
In this wild harvest, laughter we reap.

Colorful Reveries under the Sun

Under the bright beams where the colors clash,
We gather and giggle in a splattered splash.
Purple hats worn askew on our heads,
Sweet dreams of fruit dance as we tread.

Watermelon slices, a juicy delight,
Seed spitting contests take flight in our sight.
Orange zesty giggles fuse with the breeze,
As sunburned noses beg for some peace.

We sip on smoothies, tasting the fun,
It's a carnival frenzy under the sun!
With laughter like bubbles, we float and we sway,
In this colorful maze, come join us and play!

A picnic spread wide with wild juicy charms,
Grapes like cannonballs spring from our arms.
Every moment a canvas of bright, silly glee,
In this kaleidoscope, let your spirit run free.

Juicy Moments

Beneath the sun where the laughter flows,
A treasure trove of gummy prose.
Cherries chime in a fruity rhyme,
Sippin' on juice, we're lost in time.

Pineapple hats and coconut pools,
We splash and we laugh, with no summer rules.
The squishy crunch of fresh fruit pies,
Socks on our hands, we bake to the skies.

Every bite a party, each squeeze a delight,
Sticky fingers dance in the golden light.
With friends all around, we giggle and munch,
In juicy moments, life's a fruit punch!

The sun starts to set but we're not yet done,
The best tales are shared when the day's just begun.
So here's to the flavors, the fun, and the cheer,
In juicy moments, happiness is near!

Sweet Sunlit Serenades

In the fields where the sunshine plays,
We sing silly tunes on warm summer days.
Honey-dripped whispers float in the air,
With giggles and joy, we banish despair.

Popsicles wobble on colorful sticks,
We chase after ice cream and all its sweet tricks.
Under bright umbrellas, we sway side to side,
In this sunny serenade, we take joy in the ride.

Peaches and cream make our taste buds burst,
Lollipops twirl as we quench our thirst.
With every note, laughter swells high,
In sweetness and cheer, we let out a sigh.

A serenade of flavor, a musical show,
Let's dance with the fruit, let our happiness flow!
With every swirl, a delightful refrain,
In our sunlit world, there's nothing to feign.

Sunkissed Journeys

Under the sun, we trod with glee,
Chasing shadows, just you and me.
With fruity hats and smiles so wide,
We bounced along the grassy slide.

A picnic spread with colors bright,
Odd sandwiches took off in flight.
Laughter echoed, birds did sing,
Oh, the joy that summer brings!

Juicy stains on shirts we wear,
How did we get jelly in our hair?
But with each slip, we just delight,
Life's a comedy, shining bright.

As sun sets low, we dance and twirl,
With watermelon hats, we give a whirl.
In every chuckle, the warmth remains,
Sunkissed journeys, joy outweighs pains.

Vibrant Vistas

Hiking hills with frosty drinks,
The forest whispers, nature winks.
Behind every tree, a giggle plays,
As we chase squirrels through leafy maze.

Oh, the sights, like summer's dream,
A burst of colors, nature's theme.
With butterflies that dance and swirl,
We laugh as we watch them twirl!

Atop the peak, we take a break,
Snap a pic, then eat the cake.
Oh, that frosting gave a fight,
Now my nose is creamified white!

As dusk sets in, our journey's end,
We share the tales with friend to friend.
In vibrant vistas, smiles ignite,
Memories made all the long night.

Bountiful Harvests

In the orchard, we laugh and play,
Picking fruits, it's a sweet buffet.
With sticky fingers and cheeks like red,
We race for apples, it's chaos instead!

A basket full, but oh, what luck,
The pie's not safe, we've had bad luck.
Mom's recipe's toast with jam on top,
The moment we hear that delicious plop!

Flavors blend in the sunny heat,
A battle of who can eat the most sweet!
With berry stains on our clothes, we cheer,
To harvest time, we raise a beer!

When dusk arrives, we gather round,
A bonfire's spark, joy abounds.
Bountiful harvests bring delight,
As laughter echoes into the night.

Radiance in Every Bite

Sweets and treats at every stand,
A colorful feast, just as we planned.
Cupcakes twinkle with frosting bright,
Each bite is a giggle wrapped tight.

Ice cream drips on this summer day,
A fashion choice, why should I pay?
In the chaos, a cone goes flying,
But who can resist? That's worth trying!

With every flavor, smiles explode,
Tasting dreams on this laughter road.
Cherries on top make the fun ignite,
Radiance glows, a pure delight!

So let's raise our spoons and forks, my friend,
In every morsel, the joy won't end.
For in this feast, through every bite,
Life's radiant laughter shines so bright!

Shades of Juicy Joy

In the garden of laughter, we trip and we slip,
With each little berry, we savor the quip.
Juice drips down our chins, a delightful parade,
As we munch on the fruit, not a moment delayed.

Splatters of colors, from purple to red,
It's a riot of flavors, oh, what have we fed?
Chasing the sweetness, in a playful race,
We're sticky and messy, but who cares about grace!

Crimson stains linger, they tickle our glee,
With laughter and giggles, we're wild and we're free.
Forks in our hands, not a worry in sight,
Let's dance in the sunshine, till it's time for the night.

So join in the frolic, with fruits flying high,
For we're all just kids, reaching up to the sky.
These moments we treasure, so silly and bright,
In shades of pure joy, everything feels right.

Festive Flavors of Friendship

In a bowl of delight, we mix and we blend,
With flavors that spark, and smiles that extend.
A dash of good humor, a sprinkle of cheer,
Our laughter's the feast, can't you hear us near?

Friends gathered 'round, with berry-stained hands,
Creating a chaos that nobody plans.
With giggles and snorts, we munch through it all,
Each bite tells a story, we're having a ball!

Whipped cream at the ready, fumble with glee,
It's not just the taste, it's the joy that we see.
Each fruit is a friend, in this tasty embrace,
A flavor so festive, it lights up the place.

So let's clink our spoons, to memories made,
In bowls of enchantment, where friendships won't fade.
For laughter and joy are the sweetest of finds,
As we feast on the flavors, forever entwined.

Trails of Luscious Memories

On a path paved with sweetness, we wander and roam,
Each luscious bite takes us far from our home.
With fruitylicious tales on a sun-soaked day,
We dance through the berries, come what may!

Each plump little morsel, a story it brings,
Echoes of laughter, on soft fluttering wings.
The trails we have wandered, sticky and bright,
Leave footprints of joy in the shimmering light.

Oh, the squishy adventures, the giggles that flow,
As we glide down this journey, with faces aglow.
With each juicy treasure, we'munch on the past,
Savoring moments, making memories vast.

So join in the frolic, let fingers get messy,
It's these trails of delight that keep our hearts zesty.
In the land of delicious, where memories ignite,
We'll gather our laughter, and savor the bite.

Bliss in Every Bite

With a wink and a chuckle, let's dive in deep,
To the feast of sweet wonders that make our hearts leap.
Each ripe little flavor holds laughter galore,
As we gobble and munch, wanting just a bit more!

Splatters of sunshine, oh what a delight,
These tastes are the giggles that bloom in the night.
From tart to the sweet, we're a raucous brigade,
Munching on morsels, let no fun evade!

With friends gathered 'round, and plates piled high,
We share all the treasures, and let out a sigh.
For every small berry has stories to share,
Of laughter and joy, floating free in the air.

So lift up your fork, let's toast to this feast,
To all of the joys, may they never cease!
In each scrumptious moment, pure bliss we incite,
Let's cherish the flavors found in every bite!

A Taste of the Wild

In the forest, I found a bush,
With colors so vivid, it made me hush.
I plucked a few, gave them a try,
Then danced around like I could fly.

The squirrels laughed, they called me a clown,
As I wore juice stains like a berry crown.
I slipped on a leaf, oh what a sight,
Rolling down hills, a hilarious flight.

Nature's candy, I can't resist,
With every sweet nibble, I'm in a twist.
The taste is wild, but what's wildest still,
Are the goofy faces I make at will.

So join me here in this fruity spree,
Where laughter and berries grow wild and free.
A taste of the wild, come take your bite,
And giggle along till the fall of night.

Bliss in Every Drop

I found a jar of goo so bright,
With flavors that took me to new heights.
I spread it thick on toast one morn,
Then slipped and fell, oh what a scorn!

Sticky fingers and million laughs,
Chasing kids and their fruity gaffs.
We made a mess, but who would care?
We laughed so hard, it filled the air.

Each drop a burst of happiness so grand,
I am the jam, and here's my stand.
I'll juggle jars and leap with glee,
As apples sing, and the plums will agree.

So dip a spoon and take a dive,
In this wide world where flavors thrive.
Bliss in every drop, come take a sip,
Just mind the floor before you slip!

Sunlit Explorer

Under the sun, I roam around,
With a basket of treasures that I found.
Each fruit glistens, a saucy delight,
I smile at shadows, they giggle in fright.

I climbed a tree to snag the best,
But lost my grip, oh what a jest!
Fell in a patch of soft juicy treats,
With flavor explosions that can't be beat.

I danced like a fool with strawberry shoes,
While sharing my finds with the local moose.
We swapped stories of sun and fun,
Until we noticed we baked like a bun.

So let's raise a toast to our fruity quests,
With sweet laughter that never rests.
Sunlit explorations with every bite,
In this wild adventure, everything's right.

Fantasies in Flavor

In a land where fruits dance and sway,
Giggling plums rule the ballet.
With cherries that chuckle and raspberries grin,
They invite us all to join in their spin.

A castle of cake with frosting galore,
Where laughter echoes, just walk through the door.
I plopped on a slice and giggled so loud,
The jelly moat welcomed the zaniest crowd.

Marshmallow clouds in the dessert sky,
We bounce on these treats, oh my, oh my!
With every bite, our dreams take flight,
In a world of flavor, hearts ignite.

So gather your friends for this wild spree,
Where fantasies bloom underneath the berry tree.
In laughter and treats, we'll always find,
The sweet, silly joys that life's designed.

Plump Whispers

In the garden where laughter grows,
Fuzzy friends dance, nobody knows.
Chasing shadows, they slip and slide,
Jam on our fingers, we're filled with pride.

A plump one bounces, oh so round,
Rolling away, it won't be found.
Giggling echoes fill the warm air,
Silly antics, without a care.

Splashed in sun, what a sight to see,
Chubby delights playing hide and seek.
Folk gather 'round with baskets in hand,
To savor the spoils from this jolly land.

As twilight falls, we caper and play,
In this fruity realm, we'll forever stay.
With each juicy bite, we laugh and cheer,
In this merry orchard, full of cheer.

Berries Beneath Blue Skies

Under the sun, we frolic and roam,
A berry patch feels just like home.
Wobbling bodies and sticky grins,
Laughter erupts as the fun begins.

Caps on heads, we're dressed for the quest,
Plucking the fruits, we're doing our best.
Giggling, we slip on leaves and mud,
Our playful hearts are never to bud.

Sunshine paints us bright and bold,
As stories of treasure and mischief unfold.
Each berry plucked brings a hilarious tale,
Of spills and slips on a fruity trail.

With belly laughs echoing far and wide,
We celebrate life with nature as our guide.
In the patch of joy, we twirl and spin,
Under the light, our fun can begin.

Tasting the Day's Joys

From dawn till dusk, we munch away,
Each tiny fruit brings a bright ballet.
With cheeks like pillows, round and sweet,
Every nibble feels like a treat.

The picnic spread with colors so bold,
Tart and sweet stories waiting to be told.
We toast with glasses of wild grape juice,
Sipping slowly, releasing our moose.

Fingers stained with nature's own art,
Making memories, that's just the start.
The day winds down, but what a delight,
As dusk whispers sweetly, we spark the night.

In laughter and joy, we find our way,
Tasting life's wonders, come what may.
With each little bite, we savor and cheer,
Let's make moments of fun last all year.

Nature's Palette

A splash of color, a burst of fun,
Under the sun, our hearts shall run.
Juicy treasures await our hands,
Art in the fields, in nature's lands.

Painting our faces with blueberry hues,
Splattering joy, like tangoing blues.
Wandering wild, what an amusing ride,
In a landscape where giggles abide.

With bowls overflowing, we all join in,
Creating a feast with big silly grins.
The laughter ripples like rivers run,
As we share the giggles, it's never done.

Under the canvas of sunlit skies,
We relish each moment, no need for disguise.
With nature's palette, we dance and sway,
Finding our joy in a fruity ballet.

Sweet Escape

In a patch so bright and sweet,
The fruit parade can't be beat.
With laughter bouncing off each bush,
We race each other in a rush.

Jelly stains on every shirt,
Chasing nectar, feeling hurt.
Splatters, giggles, sticky hands,
Life's a party in these lands.

Forgotten shoes are left behind,
A fruity frenzy, so unrefined.
Frolicking 'neath the sunny sky,
We won't stop until we cry!

With each surefire slip and trip,
Our joy spills out like a wild quip.
The sweetest laughs on our lips,
A moment ripe, the world eclipsed.

Rhythm of the Orchard

A beat that's fresh, a dance so free,
We shimmy near the apple tree.
Twist and twirl with joyful flair,
The fruits around us show we care.

Silly steps and fruity tunes,
Underneath the playful moons.
We swing and sway, the ground is a stage,
Nature's concert, heart uncaged.

A stumble here, a giggle there,
Our legs entwined, hands in the air.
We harvest laughs with every spin,
Until the orchard's fun begins.

With pies and puns, we fill the air,
An orchard caper, no compare.
Time stands still, our spirits lift,
Together here, the sweetest gift.

Melodies of the Meadow

In the meadow where we roam,
Laughter echoes, feeling home.
The daisies hum a joyful tune,
As we skip 'neath the glowing moon.

Kites take flight, we run around,
With snacks hidden, adventure found.
Giggles dance in the warm breeze,
A serenade of bumblebees.

Sprinklers spray, a water fight,
Our outfits drenched, oh what a sight!
In wild delight, we won't give in,
The sweetest chaos begins to spin.

With every hop, the meadow sings,
A symphony of crazy things.
Joy abounds in every patch,
Friendship's song, the perfect match.

Juxtaposition of Flavor

A mix of tart and sweetness bold,
In every bite, a story told.
We taste the rainbow, sip the sun,
These flavors clash, but oh what fun!

Lemon zest with berry cheer,
A burst of giggles, can't we steer?
Peachy whispers, grape's loud shout,
In our mouths, they dance about.

Sundaes piled with bright delight,
Each scoop leads to wild insight.
Chocolate, whipped cream, all in glee,
The flavor fest is wild and free.

With every drip, a grin appears,
We savor laughter, toast with cheers.
In this sweet mess, life's finest taste,
Juxtaposed joy, never in haste.

The Taste of Summer

In a patch of laughter, I sit,
Stained fingers from the juicy wit.
Each bite's a giggle, each squirt's a cheer,
Sweet sun-kissed moments, we hold dear.

A dance on tongues, flavors collide,
Comedic crunches, we just can't hide.
With every nibble, the jokes unfold,
A mouthful of laughter, a story told.

Beneath the sun, we make our stand,
Cheeks rosy-red, just as we planned.
The summer's a joke, in flavor's embrace,
Each berry's a burst, a sweet little face.

The warmth of the laughter, a sunlit spree,
With berries and buddies, wild and free.
In this fruit-filled riot, we all proclaim,
The taste of summer is a silly game.

Ripe Reflections

In the orchard of jokes, we find our peace,
Ripe with the laughter, may it never cease.
A slip on the ground, a tumble, a fall,
Echoes of chuckles against the tall.

Pies in the making, disasters await,
With sticky fingers, we tempt our fate.
A cherry on top, or a face full of goo,
What's life without laughter, a wild hullabaloo?

Each plump little fruit carries stories untold,
Of mishaps and giggles and friendships bold.
A reflection of sunbeams and funny delight,
In this harvest of chaos, everything's bright.

With whispers of sweetness, we gather around,
A festival of chuckles, in laughter we drown.
So come take a bite, let the stories unfold,
In ripe reflections, our joy's manifold.

A Harvest of Happiness

Wandering through fields of color and cheer,
A gathering of joy, come lend me your ear.
Every slip on the ground, a comedy gold,
In this harvest of laughter, we boldly uphold.

Baskets a-brim with the zany and sweet,
We pluck at the sunshine, avoiding defeat.
Laughter's a crop that we plant in our hearts,
Growing stronger and brighter, like wild little arts.

With each little snack, the chuckles ignite,
Our picnic's a riot, a sheer, funny sight.
From the fields to the table, the giggles cascade,
In this harvest of happiness, no roles are played.

So here's to the moments, the snacks that we share,
The fruits of our labor, a sweetened affair.
Chase away worries with jests from the vine,
In this festival of laughter, everything's fine.

Sunkissed Delights

Beneath the blue skies, we gather and grin,
With cheeks stuffed like chipmunks, that's how we begin.

Grapes rolling down, like a silly parade,
In this sun-kissed delight, let's go get laid.

Ripe fruits like jewels, with a jingle they bounce,
Each squirt brings a laugh, like a friend with a flounce.
Splatters and sprays, the hilarity blooms,
We're turning the picnic into carnival rooms.

The flavor's outrageous, the fun never stops,
With berries so juicy, we dance on the tops.
Sunkissed and happy, we raise a toast high,
To humor in harvest, as kite tails fly.

So come share the giggles, let laughter not fade,
In these sunkissed delights, our memories are laid.
With every sweet bite, our joy intertwines,
In this land of the funny, happiness shines.

www.ingramcontent.com/pod-product-compliance
Lightning Source LLC
Chambersburg PA
CBHW051731290426
43661CB00122B/223